DIE
HARD

ARD

THE AUTHORIZED COLORING AND ACTIVITY BOOK

DOOGIE HORNER

HARPER
DESIGN
An Imprint of HarperCollins Publishers

DIE HARD: THE AUTHORIZED COLORING AND ACTIVITY BOOK
Copyright © 2016 Die Hard™ © 2016 Twentieth Century Fox Film Corporation.

HarperCollins books may be purchased for educational, business,
or sales promotional use. For information please email the
Special Markets Department at SPsales@harpercollins.com.

Published in 2016 by
Harper Design
An Imprint of HarperCollins*Publishers*
195 Broadway
New York, NY 10007
Tel: (212) 207-7000
Fax: (855) 746-6023
harperdesign@harpercollins.com
www.hc.com

Distributed throughout the world by
HarperCollins Publishers
195 Broadway
New York, NY 10007

ISBN 978-0-06-249230-2

Cover design and illustration by Doogie Horner

Printed in the United States of America

First Printing, 2016

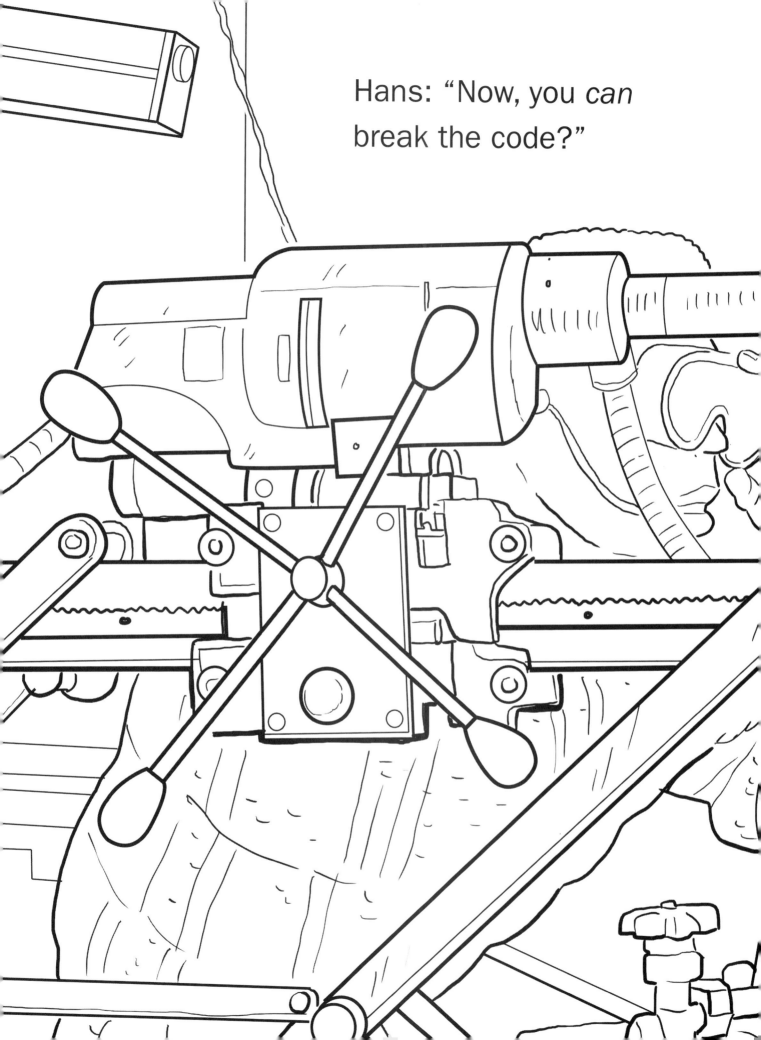

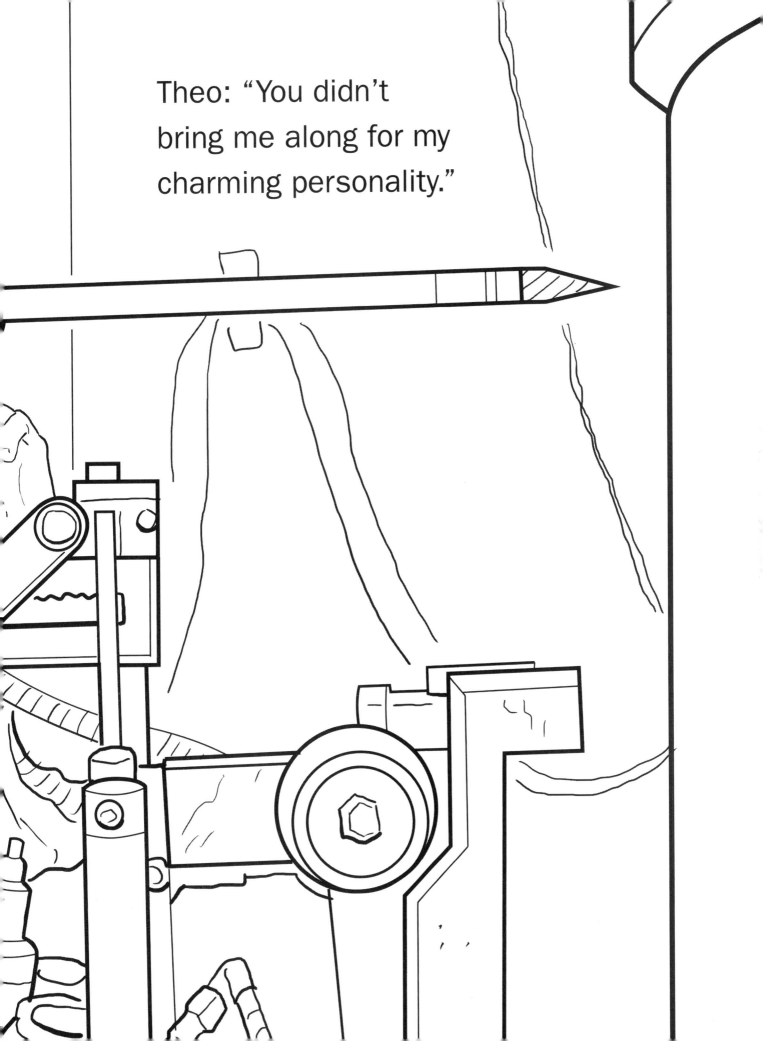

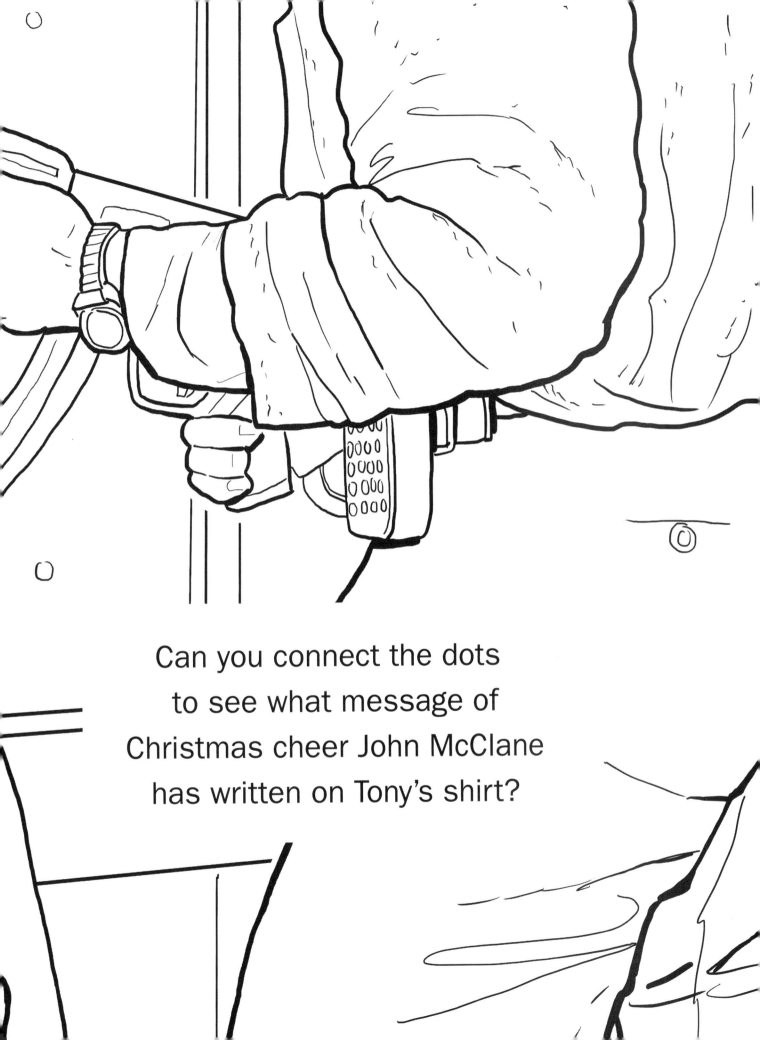

Can you connect the dots
to see what message of
Christmas cheer John McClane
has written on Tony's shirt?

John just killed Karl's brother.
Draw Karl's face to show how
he feels about that.

Die Hard needs to air on network TV tonight, but the movie has too much cursing! Can you help the censors seamlessly edit the offensive words from the dialogue?

911 operator: [as McClane tries to call the police] Attention, whoever you are, this channel is reserved for emergency calls only.

John McClane: No _____ (adjective) _____ (noun), lady. Do I sound like I'm ordering a pizza?

Hans Gruber: Do you really think you have a chance against us, Mr. Cowboy?

John McClane: Yippee-kai-yay, _____. (compound noun)

Dwayne T. Robinson: This is Deputy Chief of Police Dwayne T. Robinson, and I am in charge of this situation.

John McClane: Oh, you're in charge? Well, I got some bad news for you *Dwayne*. From up here it doesn't look like you're in charge of jack _____ (noun).

Dwayne T. Robinson: You listen to me, you little _____ (noun), I'm—

John McClane: _____ (previous noun)? I'm not the one who just got _____ (body part)- _____ (verb ending in -ed) on

national TV, *Dwayne*. Now, you listen to me, _____ (noun ending in -off), if you're not a part of the solution, you're a part of the problem. Quit being a part of the _____ (adjective) problem and put the other guy back on!

John McClane: [fighting Karl] _____ (compound noun), I'm going to kill you! I'm going to _____ (verb ending in -ing) cook you. I'm going to _____ (verb ending in -ing) eat you!

Big Johnson: [flying in the helicopter to the roof] Just like _____ (adjective) Saigon, hey, Slick?

Little Johnson: I was in junior high, _____ (body part) _____ (body part).

Hans Gruber: This time John Wayne does not walk off into the sunset with Grace Kelly.

John McClane: That was Gary Cooper, _____ (very specific body part).

"Come out to the coast. We'll get together, have a few laughs . . ."

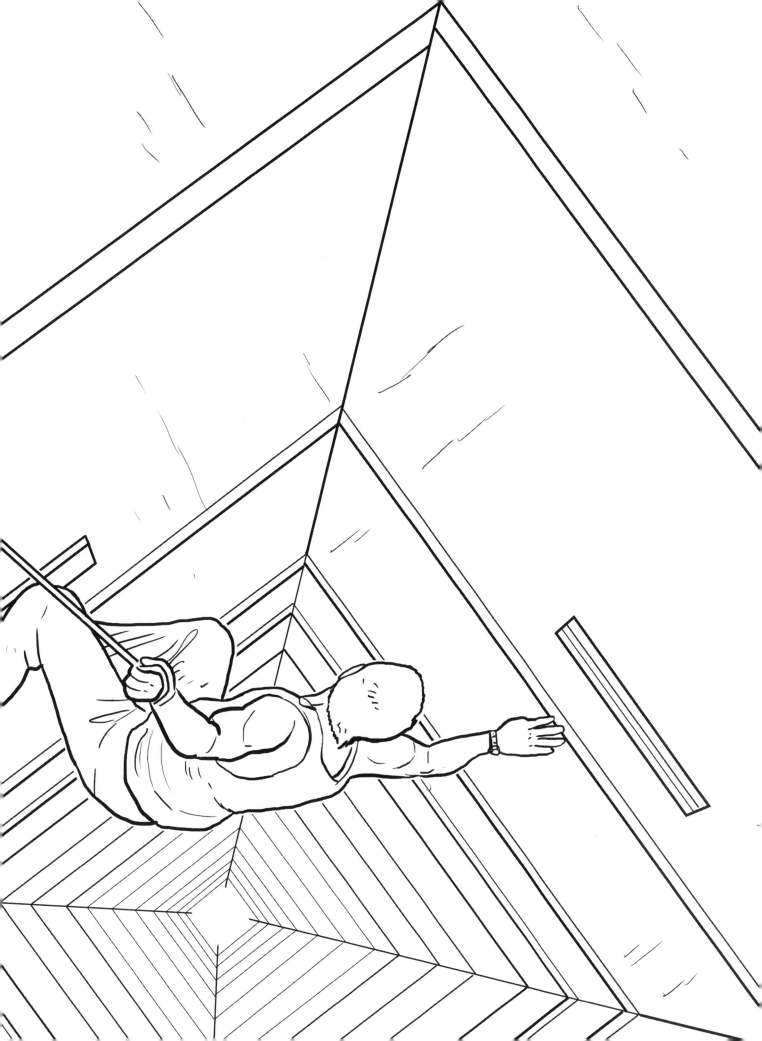

John McClane's feet hurt. Can you help him find a matching pair of shoes? (Solution on last page.)

BINGO HARD

Just when you thought *Die Hard* couldn't get more exciting, now you can play bingo while you watch it!

Is that . . . Huey Lewis?	man with a ponytail	Twinkies	John quotes W.C. Fields	Karl flips out
Deputy Police Chief Dwayne Robinson gets belittled	sleigh bells on soundtrack	pregnant woman	terrorist eats candy bar	boobs
Beethoven on soundtrack	John kills someone without shooting them	Explosion	bonsai tree	Ellis tries to speak German
fashion talk	samurai statue	Stevie Wonder joke	headshot	Hans Gruber smiles
exploding hockey puck thingie	cigarette break	Bach on soundtrack	bromance	close up of a Rolex

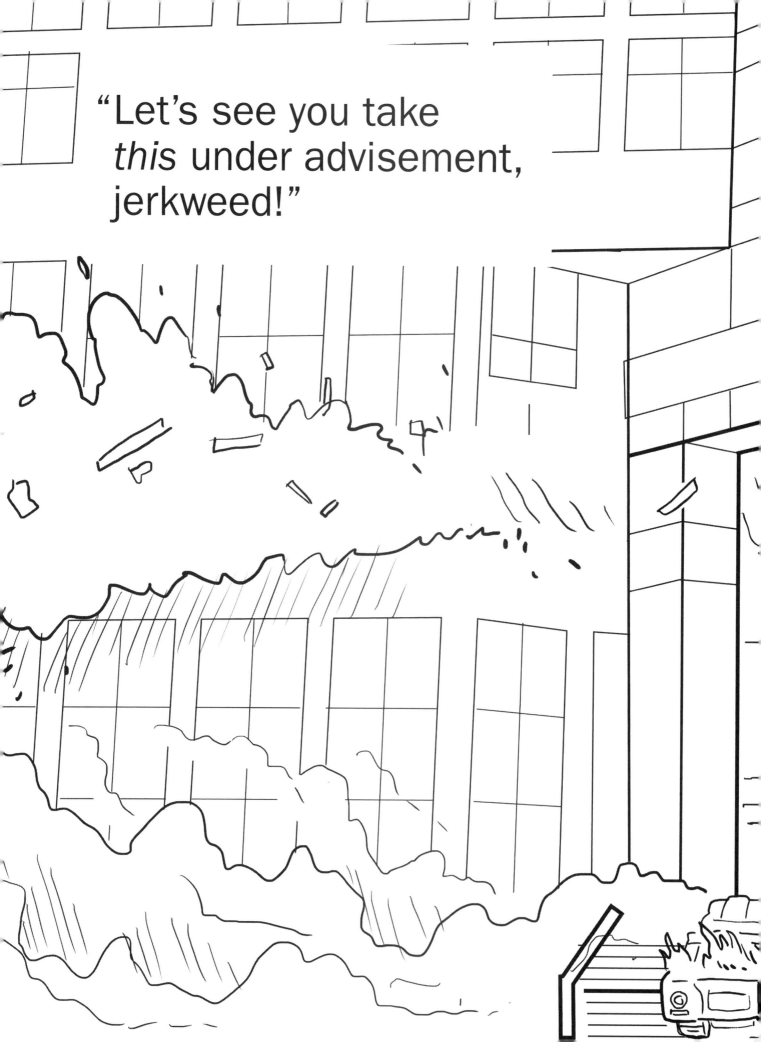

"Hey, *sprechen Sie* talk? . . .
Hans, bubbe, I'm your white knight."

ENTER

There's glass all over the floor, and poor John McClane isn't wearing any shoes! Can you help him get to the exit without cutting his feet?

(Solution on last page.)

EXIT

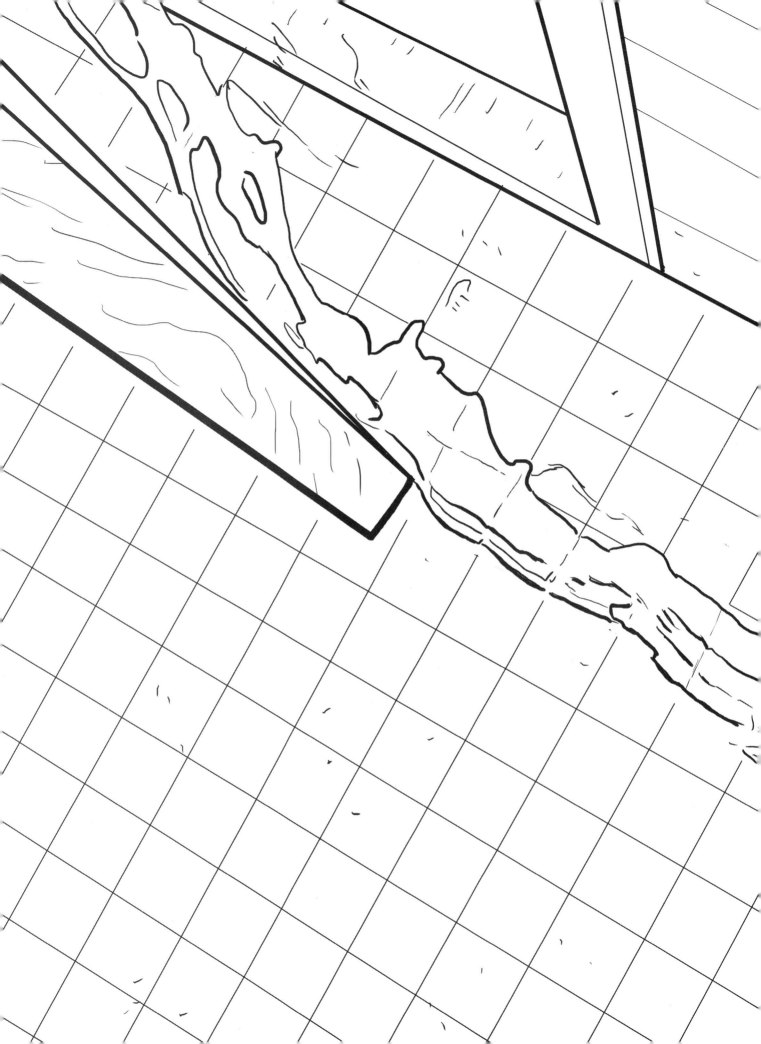

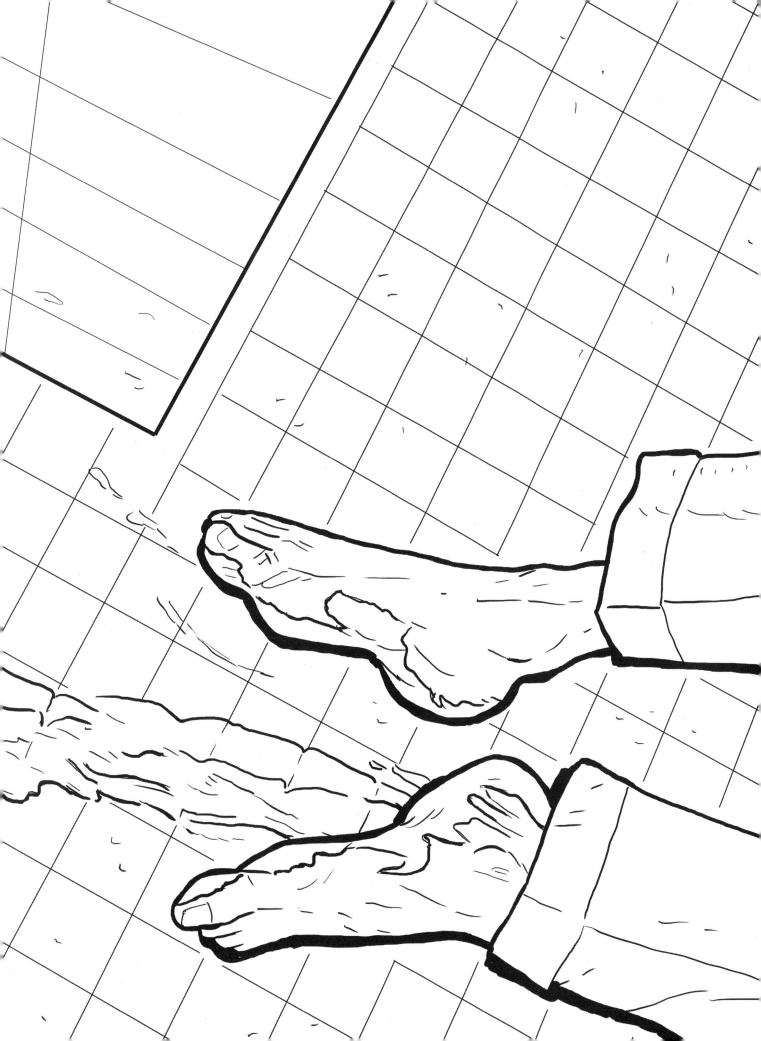

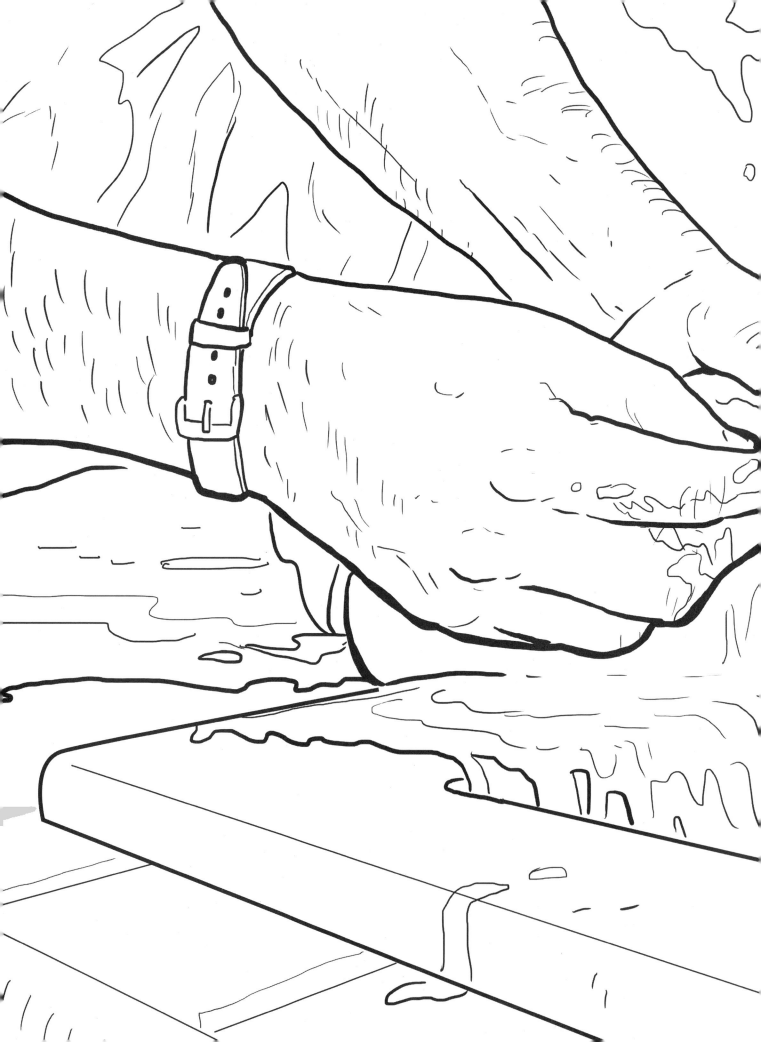

"All things being equal,
   I'd rather be in Philadelphia."

C-4 EXPLOSIVES C-4

Hans wants to blow the roof, but he doesn't know which detonator button is connected to the C-4. Can you help him choose the right one?

(Solution on last page.)

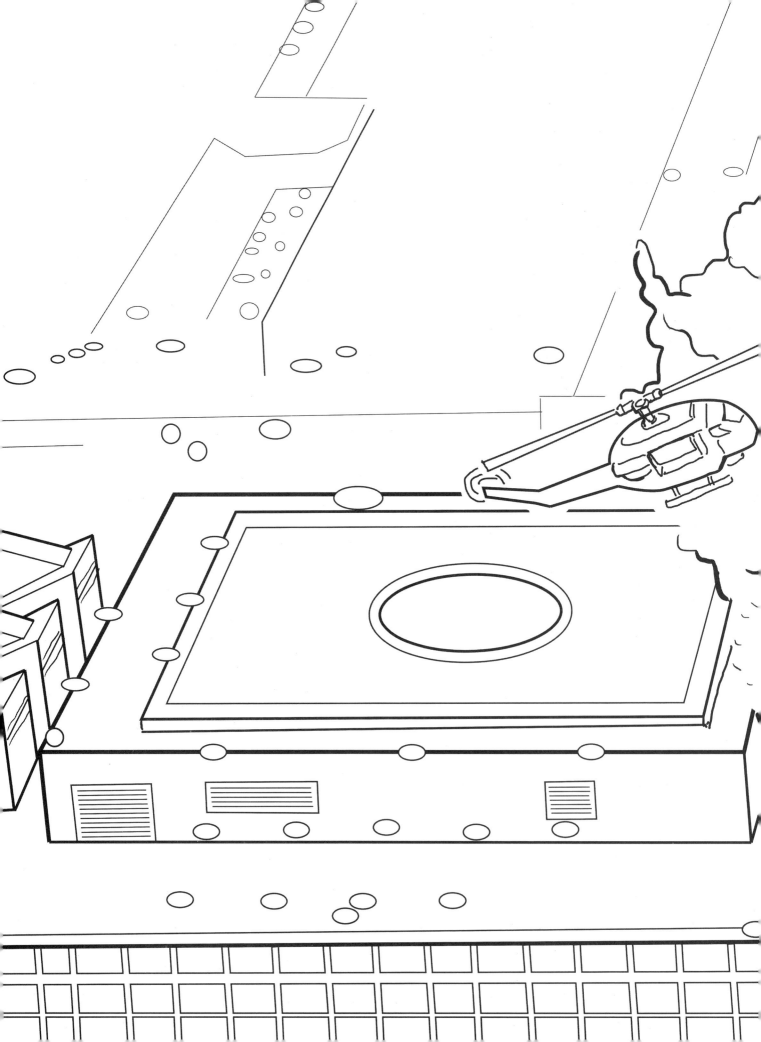

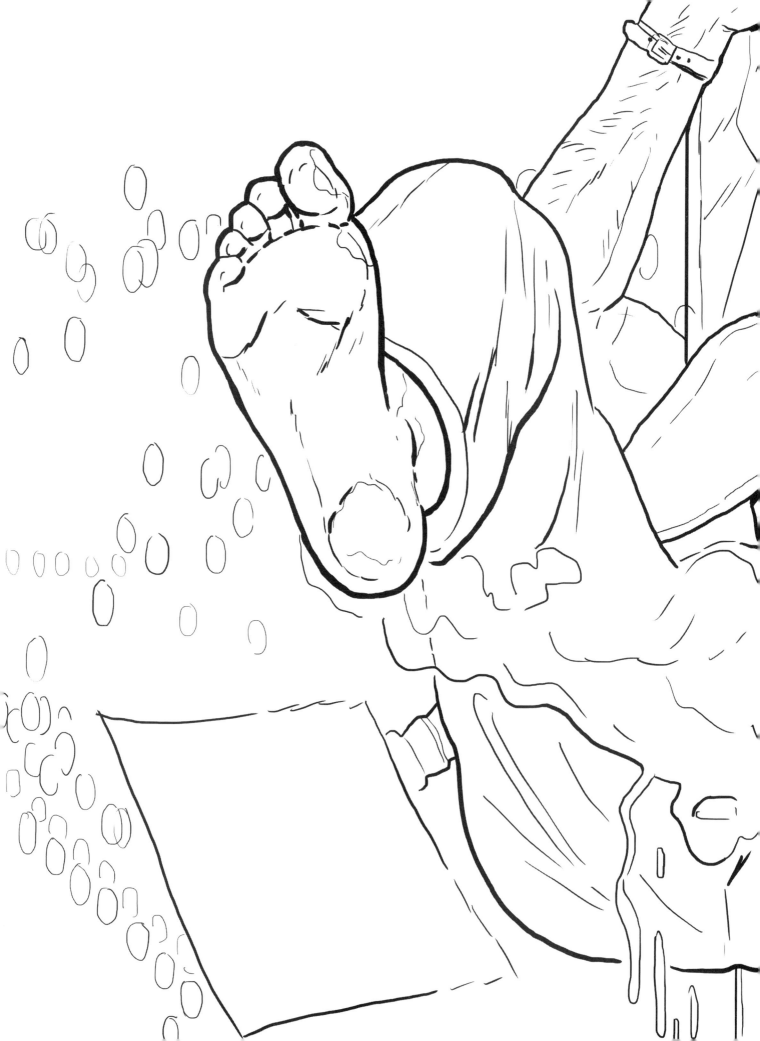

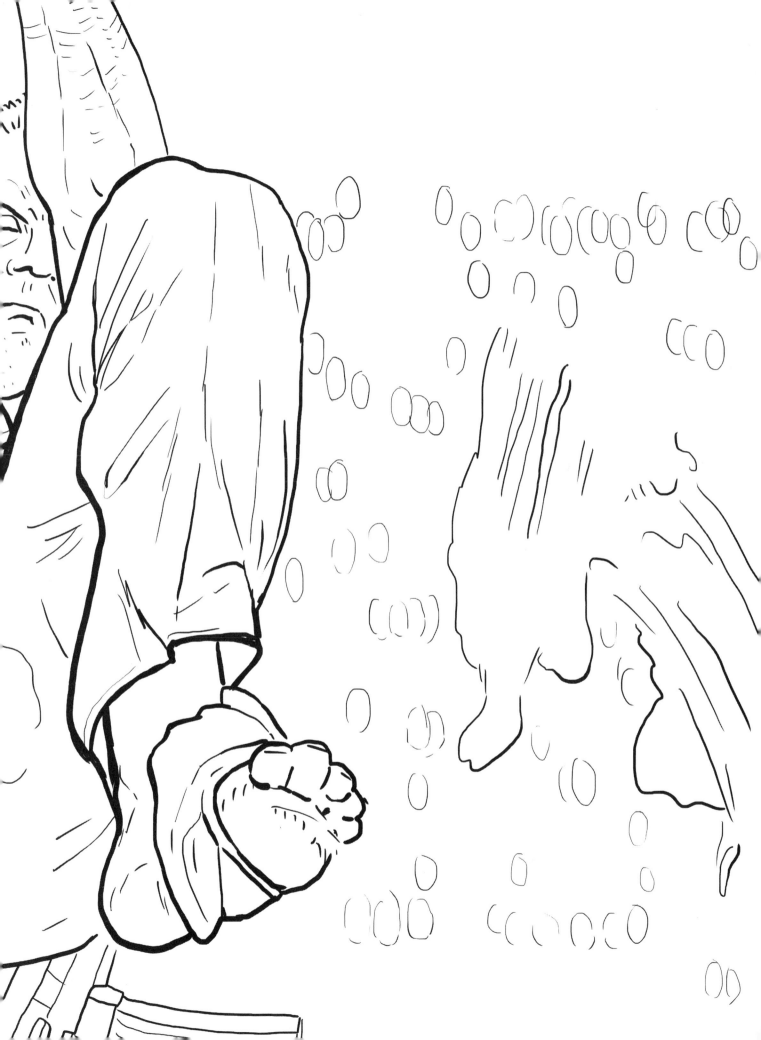

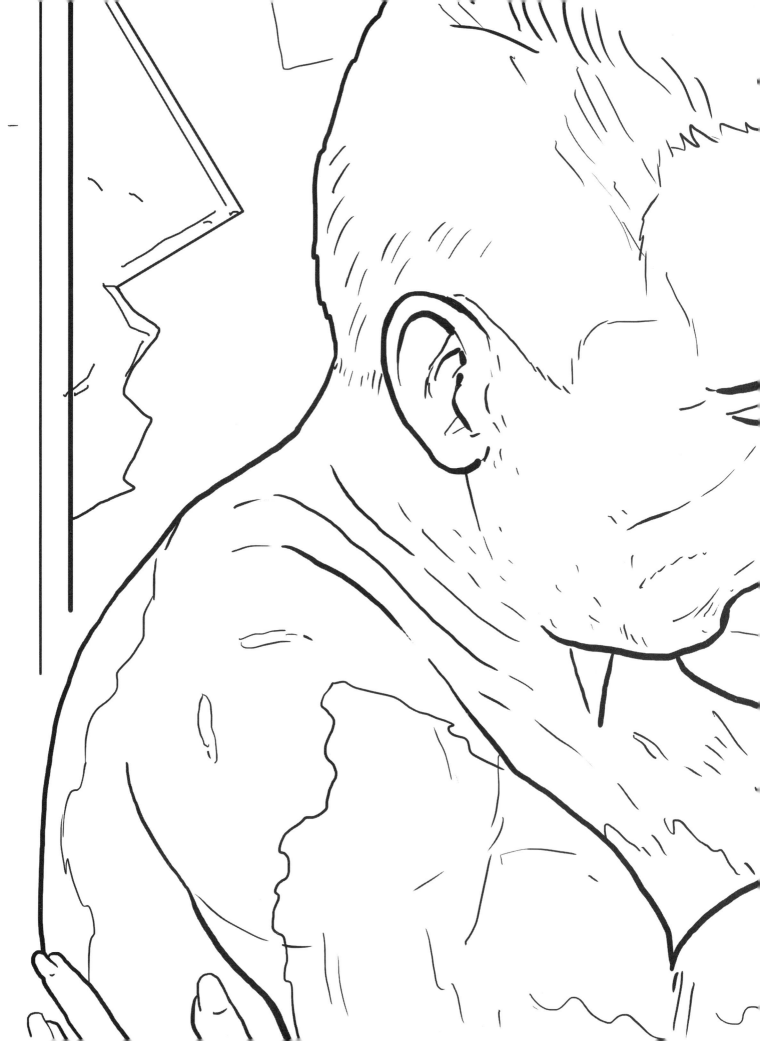

PUZZLE SOLUTIONS

Matching shoes: Unfortunately for John McClane, none of these shoes match.

Glass maze: There is no way to get to the exit without walking through the glass. I'm sorry, John. I know you just wanted to have a quiet holiday with your estranged family, maybe try to patch things up, but it looks like this just isn't your day. Hang in there, buddy.

Hans blows the roof: The correct button is detonator button 3, and I'm a little surprised that you're helping Hans like this. Whose side are you on?

ABOUT THE ILLUSTRATOR

Doogie Horner watched *Die Hard* so many times, he was able to draw this book entirely from memory. He's convinced that Holly's Rolex is a symbol of her career, and that (spoiler alert) when John unclasps it at the end—plummeting Hans to his death—it's a metaphor for Holly giving up her career to spend more time with her family. He's not sure how he feels about that.

Doogie's previous books include *Everything Explained Through Flowcharts*, *100 Ghosts*, and *Some Very Interesting Cats Perhaps You Weren't Aware Of*. He also has a comedy album called *A Delicate Man*. He lives in New York City with his wife and son, whom he would gladly walk over broken glass to save. You can learn more at www.doogiehorner.com.